LOOKING AFTER YOUR PET

Guinea Pig

Text by Clare Hibbert

Photography by Robert and Justine Pickett

HODDER
Wayland

an imprint of Hodder Children's Books

Titles in the LOOKING AFTER YOUR PET series:

• Cat • Dog • Hamster • Rabbit
• Guinea Pig • Fish

© 2004 White-Thomson Publishing Ltd

Produced by White-Thomson Publishing Ltd
2/3 St Andrew's Place, Lewes, BN7 1UP

Editor: Elaine Fuoco-Lang
Inside design: Leishman Design
Cover design: Hodder Wayland
Photographs: Robert Pickett
Proofreader: Alison Cooper

Published in Great Britain in 2004 by Hodder
Wayland, an imprint of Hodder Children's Books.

Hodder Children's Books
An imprint of Hodder Headline Limited
338 Euston Road, London, NW1 3BH

British Library Cataloguing in Publication Data
Hibbert, Clare
    Guinea pig. - (Looking after your pet)
    1.Guinea pigs as pets - Juvenile literature
    I.Title
    636.9'3592

ISBN 0 7502 4304 X

Acknowledgements
The publishers would like to thank the following
for their assistance with this book:
The PDSA (Reg. Charity 283483) for their help
and assistance with the series.

With kind thanks for guinea pigs to
Rosie Pilbeam and The Animal Care Unit,
Canterbury College.

The website addresses (URLs) included in this
book were valid at the time of going to press.
However, because of the nature of the Internet,
it is possible that some addresses may have
changed, or sites may have changed or closed
down since publication. While the author,
packager and publisher regret any inconvenience
that this may cause readers, no responsibility for
any such changes can be accepted by either the
author, the packager or the publisher.

Printed in China

Contents

Keeping guinea pigs

The first question to ask yourself is "Why do I want guinea pigs?"

Guinea pigs can be shy at first, but they make great pets. When they get to know you, they love being cuddled. But before you decide guinea pigs are the pets for you, check you will be able to look after them. You will have to buy a comfortable hutch, and a run so they can play in the garden.

▶ You will need to handle your pet guinea pig every day.

4

Guinea pigs with rough or long hair need daily grooming.

Top Tips

🐾 Do you want guinea pigs with short, rough or long hair? They all make wonderful pets!

🐾 You will need to keep more than one guinea pig, or it may get lonely.

🐾 Never keep males and females together. You will end up with lots of baby guinea pigs.

Guinea pigs usually live to be four or five, but can live to be as old as eight. You will need to feed and handle your pets every day for all those years. You will also need to clean out their hutch, and find someone to look after them when you go on holiday.

Two guinea pigs are better than one. They will keep each other company.

5

Choosing your pets

Buy healthy baby guinea pigs.

First, decide where to get your guinea pigs. Try a pet shop, breeder or animal shelter. Or maybe you know someone who has baby guinea pigs, called puppies, in need of a good home. It is best to get young guinea pigs that are five to six weeks old.

▼ Take your time when you go to choose your guinea pigs. Make sure you pick the liveliest puppies of the litter.

ask to handle the guinea pigs so that you can check they are in good health. If you are choosing two pigs, make sure they are either males (boars) or females (sows) from the same litter. If you want more than two, choose sows they may be less likely to fight.

Find out what food your pets are used to and ask for a little of their bedding to put in their new hutch.

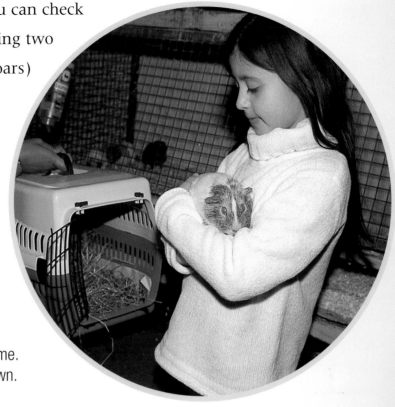

► Use an animal carrier to take your new pets home. Put some hay inside so that they can nestle down.

Top Tips

When choosing your guinea pigs, look for:

🐾 Clean, shiny fur with no bare or damp patches

🐾 A rounded, plump and firm body

🐾 Shiny eyes and clean nose, ears and mouth

🐾 Liveliness!

► See how this guinea pig's eyes shine! A healthy, alert animal like this one will make a wonderful pet.

7

A home for your pets

Have a hutch ready for your new guinea pigs.

For two pigs, the hutch should be at least 60 cm long, 40 cm wide and 40 cm high. It needs a dark sleeping area and a daytime area with a wire-mesh door to let in light and air. The hutch should also be raised off the ground, on legs or bricks, to keep out the damp. It is best to put the hutch indoors – a shed is ideal.

▲ When you get your new pets home, put them straight into their hutch. Stay low to the ground when handling guinea pigs. A high fall could kill them.

When the weather is not too cold, you can put the hutch outside. Make sure the hutch is properly weatherproofed, though, and put it somewhere that is shaded from the sun and sheltered from the wind.

Top Tips

Weather beaters

🐾 If the hutch is outside, cover it with a sheet of plastic when there is heavy rain. Make sure you remove it and check for damp after a heavy shower.

🐾 Never put the hutch in a garage used by cars. Petrol fumes could kill your pets.

🐾 Do not put the hutch in a greenhouse. Your pets could overheat and die.

▲ Your new pets will want to explore their surroundings. Leave them alone for a few hours while they get used to their new home.

▼ Guinea pigs cannot stand too much cold – or too much heat. Put your pets' hutch outside only in mild weather and make sure there is some shelter from the sun.

Inside the hutch

Make the hutch into a cosy home for your pets.

Line the floor with sheets of newspaper. You can add wood shavings if you want, but never put sawdust in your pets' hutch – it can damage their eyes and lungs. Fill the sleeping area with shredded paper and hay. Your guinea pigs will like to eat and play with the hay, as well as sleep in it. Do not use straw instead of hay. It is cheaper, but not so good for your pets.

▼ Guinea pigs love to explore. A plastic tube makes a perfect toy.

Fix a water bottle to the mesh door and put the food bowls inside the hutch. Finally, add a fruit-tree branch for your guinea pigs to gnaw – this will keep their teeth trim.

▲ Pet guinea pigs need lots of hay to nibble. Give fresh hay every day.

Checklist: hutch kit

- Plastic drip-feed water bottle with a metal spout

- Pottery food bowls – one for dried and one for fresh food

- Bedding, such as shredded white paper

- Hay

- Sheets of old newspaper

- Fruit-tree branch or gnawing block

- Tubes or boxes to explore – cardboard is fine, or you can buy tough plastic ones

- Wood shavings

11

Feeding your guinea pigs

Like you, your guinea pigs should not miss meals.

It is your job to feed your pets. Give them special guinea pig food, which is a mix of dried plants, seeds and vegetables. You must make sure they always have dried food to eat.

▲ Feeding time! Check on the packet or with your vet to find out how much dried food to give your guinea pigs.

eed your pets at the same time ach day. As well as the food mix, dd an extra handful of hay for em to nibble. For a special treat, y handfeeding some shelled, nsalted peanuts.

ating dry food is thirsty work, so eep your pets' water bottle topped p. You should also give them fresh ruit and vegetables (see page 14).

▲ Remember to refill your guinea pigs' water bottle with fresh water every day.

Top Tips

Feeding kit

🐾 Put your pets' food in heavy, pottery bowls that can not be knocked over.

🐾 Never top up the food bowl. Throw away any leftovers from the day before.

🐾 Do not put anything plastic in the hutch unless it has been specially made for guinea pigs. Your guinea pigs will gnaw it.

▶ To stay healthy, a guinea pig needs a mix of dried food, fresh hay and raw vegetables or fruit.

Get fresh!

Guinea pigs love eating fresh fruit and vegetables.

Like you, they need vitamin C, so you should give them some fresh food every day. About a handful for each pig is enough – more might give them upset tummies. Always wash any fresh food first.

Give a mix of foods. Chop up vegetables such as carrots, celery, cucumber or corn-on-the-cob. Your guinea pigs will also enjoy a small piece of apple, pear or even orange. Try hiding the fresh food and see how long it takes your pets to sniff it out. Remember where you've put it, though. You should take out any uneaten fresh food after a day, before it goes off.

▶ This guinea pig is enjoying a piece of cabbage. You will soon find out which fruits and vegetables are your pets' favourites.

Want to know a great way to make friends with your new pet? Handfeed it a slice of delicious apple!

Checklist: wild plants

You could give your guinea pigs food from the wild. Try freshly picked:

- Chickweed
- Clover
- Coltsfoot
- Dandelions
- Grass
- Groundsel
- Plantain
- Shepherd's purse
- Yarrow

Don't pick weeds from beside the road – they will have poisons on them from all the car exhausts.

Handling

Handle each of your guinea pigs every day.

For the first couple of days, just talk to your pets so that they get used to your voice. Then you can begin to handle them. Always sit down to hold a guinea pig so it is safely cradled in your lap. Cup your hands to support its body. Remember to talk softly – your pet will like the sound of your voice.

◄ Make sure your guinea pig's body i well supported and hold it close to you chest or lap.

y not to make any jerky movements
hat might startle your guinea pig.
on't handle your pets too soon after
ou have fed them. Give them time for
heir tummies to settle first.

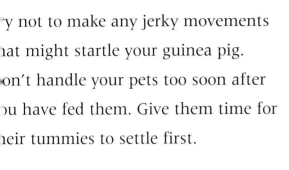

▶ Give your guinea pigs plenty of
attention each day and spend the same
amount of time handling each one.

Pet Talk

Guinea pig hairstyles

There are three types of guinea pig hair –
short, long or rough. If your guinea pig is long-
haired or rough-haired, you will need to brush
its coat every day. Short-haired pigs like being
brushed too. Get a soft baby brush and only
use it for grooming your guinea pigs.

When you groom your pet, brush
gently. Move the brush down the
back away from the head.

Great outdoors

Your guinea pigs will enjoy getting out in the fresh air.

On fine days, you can let your pets out in a triangular-shaped run called a grazing ark. First check that the grass has not been treated with weedkiller.

Choose an ark with a nesting area at one end, raised if possible. Put some hay in here, for your guinea pigs to nestle in when they want to take a nap. Move the ark around the lawn every few days, to give your guinea pigs fresh grass to nibbl They will need dried food, too, and water

▼ Put fresh hay in the ark for your guinea pigs. Guinea pigs need to have hay all the time – even when there is plenty of grass to eat!

▲ Your grazing ark should have a shaded area at one end where your pets can escape from the sun. You can let guinea pigs and rabbits share the ark, as long as you stay there to watch over them.

Pet Talk

If you also have a pet rabbit, you can put it in the grazing ark with the guinea pigs. You will need to supervise them, though, and supply them with separate food. Your rabbits and guinea pigs should not share the same hutch. They need their own space and might not get on if they are together all the time.

► Remember to fix a full water bottle to the side of the ark.

Guinea pig talk

Your guinea pigs will try to talk to you!

When your pets hear you coming, they might squeak to get your attention. They also make cooing noises to reassure each other. Listen out for purring and chirruping. Your guinea pigs make these noises when they are happy.

▶ Your guinea pig will love being stroked and may make purring noises if it is relaxed. It is a great way for you to make friends with your pet.

Pet Talk

Guinea pigs have a brilliant sense of smell. That is how they recognize each other – and you! They also mark their territory with scent. They have scent glands on their cheeks, backs and bottoms.

When guinea pigs are annoyed, they make a chattering sound. This might be a sign that your pets are going to fight. It should not happen if you choose pigs from the same litter. Another noise you might hear is a frightened squeal. If this happens when you are handling your guinea pig, gently put it back in its hutch.

▲ Guinea pigs can be real chatterboxes! Listen to the noises your pets make to each other.

▼ These guinea pigs are saying "hello!" to each other.

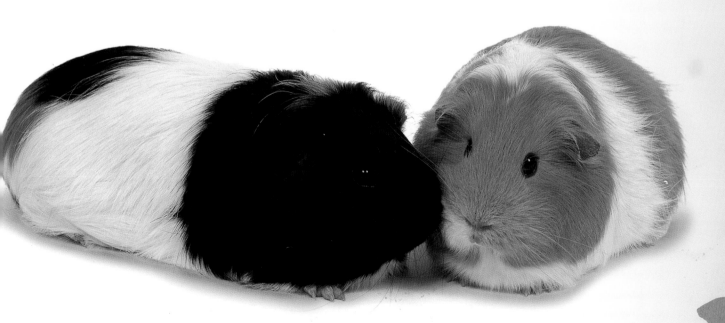

Cleaning out

Keep your guinea pig's hutch clean – or it will smell.

Check the hutch every day. You should remove any leftover food, droppings or wet bedding. Wash the food bowls and water bottle, too.

Once a week, give the hutch a proper clean. First, put your guinea pigs somewhere safe – a cardboard box or carrying case is ideal. Empty out all the hay, shredded paper and newspaper.

▲ It is a good idea to wear rubber gloves when you are cleaning out the hutch.

Brush or scrape any dirt from the floor. Now you can put down fresh newspaper and fill the nesting area with clean hay and shredded paper.

Every couple of months, scrub the hutch with special pet disinfectant. Rinse away any traces of disinfectant, then let the hutch dry out completely.

▶ Make sure the hutch is fully dry before putting down newspaper and bedding.

Checklist: cleaning kit

Only use these things for cleaning out your guinea pigs.

- Rubber gloves
- Dustpan and brush
- Scraper
- Scrubbing brush
- Plastic bowl or bucket for hot water
- Special pet disinfectant
- Washing-up liquid
- Sponge
- Bottle brush
- Teatowel or paper towels

Healthy pets

If you look after
your pets, they
will probably
stay healthy.

Although guinea pigs are
generally calm and healthy pets
you should take sick guinea pigs
to the vet as soon as possible.

Even healthy guinea pigs
need a yearly check-up
with the vet. He or she
will also cut their claws
or teeth if they have
grown too long.

▶ When you are handling
your pet, check its fur
for little insects
called mites.

It is not a good idea to try to breed guinea pigs. There are so many unwanted pets. But there is no need to have your pets neutered. Just keep them away from guinea pigs of the opposite sex.

Checklist:

If you see any of these signs of illness, take your guinea pig to the vet:

- Dull fur

- Sores on its skin

- Dirty ears or eyes

- Sneezing

- Lots of scratching

- Noisy breathing or wheezing

- Shivering

- Diarrhoea (upset tummy)

- Little insects (mites) in the fur

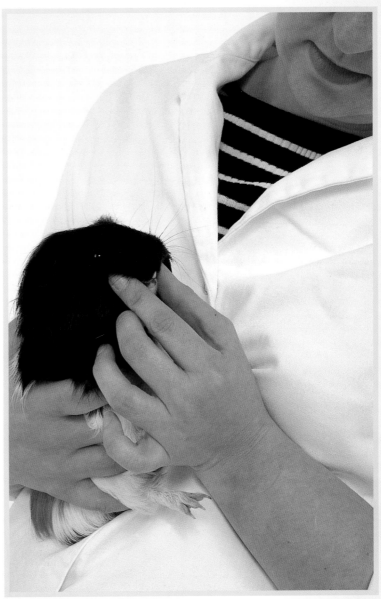

▲ Ask an adult to check your guinea pig's teeth. They should not be overgrown. If they are, you will need to take your pet to the vet.

◄ Long claws need to be cut, but this is a job for the vet. Never try to cut your pets' claws.

Holiday time

When you go on holiday, do not forget your pets.

Ask a friend to come and feed your guinea pigs once a day. They will also need to give fresh water and clean the hutch. It might be easier to take pets and all their equipment round to your friend's house.

▼ Make sure your friend knows how to look after your pet while you are away on holiday.

Write a list of what to do and add your vet's telephone number, just in case. Show your friend how to handle the pigs – gently and firmly, but without squeezing. If you cannot find anyone to care for your guinea pigs, see if your vet or local pet shop can help you.

▶ Give your friend a list of your guinea pigs' favourite foods.

Pet Talk
Meeting other animals

If your friend has guinea pigs, they will know how to look after yours. Guinea pigs do not get on with cats or dogs, though. If your friend has these, make sure they are kept away from your pets.

◀ Your pets could share a grazing ark with your friend's – as long as there is someone watching over them to check that they do not fight.

Guinea pig facts

Bet you didn't know that the Incas used to breed guinea pigs for eating! Read on for more fantastic facts

• Guinea pigs are no relation to pigs, even though the males are called boars and the females are called sows.

• Guinea pigs are rodents, related to rats and mice. Like all rodents, they have teeth that never stop growing.

• Guinea pigs are sometimes called cavies – but they don't live in caves! Their natural homes are grasslands and mountains in South America.

• Wild guinea pigs spend about six hours eating each day. They usually feed at dawn and dusk, when the dim light makes it hard for hunting animals to spot them.

• Guinea pigs sleep for about five hours a day, but they never close their eyes for more than ten minutes.

• Wild guinea pigs live in groups called colonies.

• There are around 50 different breeds of pet guinea pig.

• Mother guinea pigs grunt to call their babies.

• Unlike many rodent babies, guinea pigs are already furry when they are born – and their eyes are open, too.

Glossary

Boar
A male guinea pig.

Breeder
Someone who keeps guinea pigs to mate them and produce babies to sell. He or she will want to produce puppies of a particular breed or type.

Colony
A group of guinea pigs that live together.

Disinfectant
A cleaning fluid that kills germs. Ask your vet or pet shop for a mild disinfectant that is suitable for cleaning your guinea pigs' hutch. Follow the instructions with care.

Grazing ark
A triangular run, made of wire mesh, that you can put your guinea pigs in so that they can graze on your lawn. The ark should have a shaded area at one end, ideally raised a few centimetres off the ground to avoid damp.

Grooming
Brushing a guinea pig's fur. Long-haired or rough-haired guinea pigs need to be brushed every day.

Litter
A group of animals all born at the same time to the same mother. They are brothers and sisters.

Neutered
Removing an animal's sex organs so that it cannot have babies.

Pedigree
A particular type of guinea pig, such as an Abyssinian.

Puppy
A baby guinea pig.

Scent glands
Places on a guinea pig's body that produce a smell. Guinea pigs rub their cheeks, backs and bottoms against things to mark their territory.

Sow
A female guinea pig.

Territory
The area of land that belongs to a colony of guinea pigs.

Further information

Books

My Pet: Guinea Pig by Honor Head, photographs by Jane Burton
(Belitha Press, 2000)

Read and Wonder: I Love Guinea Pigs by Dick King-Smith,
illustrated by Anita Jeram
(Walker, 1996)

Life Cycle of a Guinea Pig by Angela Royston
(Heinemann Library, 1999)

Useful addresses

PDSA
Whitechapel Way
Priorslee
Telford
Shropshire
TF2 9PQ
Tel: 01952 290999
Fax: 01952 291035
Website: www.pdsa.org.uk

RSPCA
Wilberforce Way
Southwater
Horsham
West Sussex
RH13 9RS
Tel: 0870 3335 999
Fax: 0870 7530 284
Website: www.rspca.org.uk

Index